Agriculture

Edited by Charles A. Piddock

MEDIA ENHANCED BOOKS
AV2 BY WEIGL™
ADDED VALUE • AUDIO VISUAL

www.av2books.com

AV² provides enriched content that supplements and complements this book. Weigl's AV² books strive to create inspired learning and engage young minds in a total learning experience.

Your AV² Media Enhanced books come alive with...

Go to **www.av2books.com**, and enter this book's unique code.

BOOK CODE

K533364

AV² by Weigl brings you media enhanced books that support active learning.

Download the AV² catalog at
www.av2books.com/catalog

Audio
Listen to sections of the book read aloud.

Video
Watch informative video clips.

Embedded Weblinks
Gain additional information for research.

Try This!
Complete activities and hands-on experiments.

Key Words
Study vocabulary, and complete a matching word activity.

Quizzes
Test your knowledge.

Slide Show
View images and captions, and prepare a presentation.

... and much, much more!

AV² Online Navigation on page 48

Published by AV² by Weigl
350 5th Avenue, 59th Floor
New York, NY 10118

Websites: www.av2books.com   www.weigl.com

Library of Congress Control Number: 2014940093

ISBN 978-1-4896-1098-0 (hardcover)
ISBN 978-1-4896-1099-7 (softcover)
ISBN 978-1-4896-1100-0 (single-user eBook)
ISBN 978-1-4896-1101-7 (multi-user eBook)

Printed in the United States of America in North Mankato, Minnesota
1 2 3 4 5 6 7 8 9 0   18 17 16 15 14

052014
WEP090514

Weigl acknowledges Getty Images as its primary image supplier for this title.

Every reasonable effort has been made to trace ownership and to obtain permission to reprint copyright material. The publishers would be pleased to have any errors or omissions brought to their attention so that they may be corrected in subsequent printings.

Project Coordinator: Aaron Carr
Art Director: Terry Paulhus

Agriculture

CONTENTS

AV² Book Code 2

Introduction to Agriculture 4

History of Agriculture 6

Modern Farm Technology 14

The Global Market 22

Mapping World Agriculture 24

Future of Agriculture 32

Agriculture through History 36

Careers in Agriculture 38

Key Agricultural Organizations 40

Research an Agricultural Issue 42

Test Your Knowledge 44

Key Words 46

Index 47

Log on to www.av2books.com 48

Introduction to Agriculture

Agriculture is one of the most important human activities. People depend on it for their health, as well as for life itself. Without the food grown on the world's farms, no other human activity is possible. Over time, agricultural methods and technology have changed, and farming is much more complicated now than it was in the past. This has led to questions about whether farms can feed the planet today and if they will be able to meet the food demands of an increasing population in the future.

History of Agriculture

"Farming has undergone a number of revolutions since it was first developed by humans thousands of years ago."

Modern Farm Technology

"World food production has increased due to modern chemical **fertilizers**, intensive industrialized farming, and modern farm machines."

The Global Market

"Agriculture today is a global enterprise, influenced by large multinational companies."

Future of Agriculture

"The biggest challenge for farming in the future is growing enough food to feed an expanding world population."

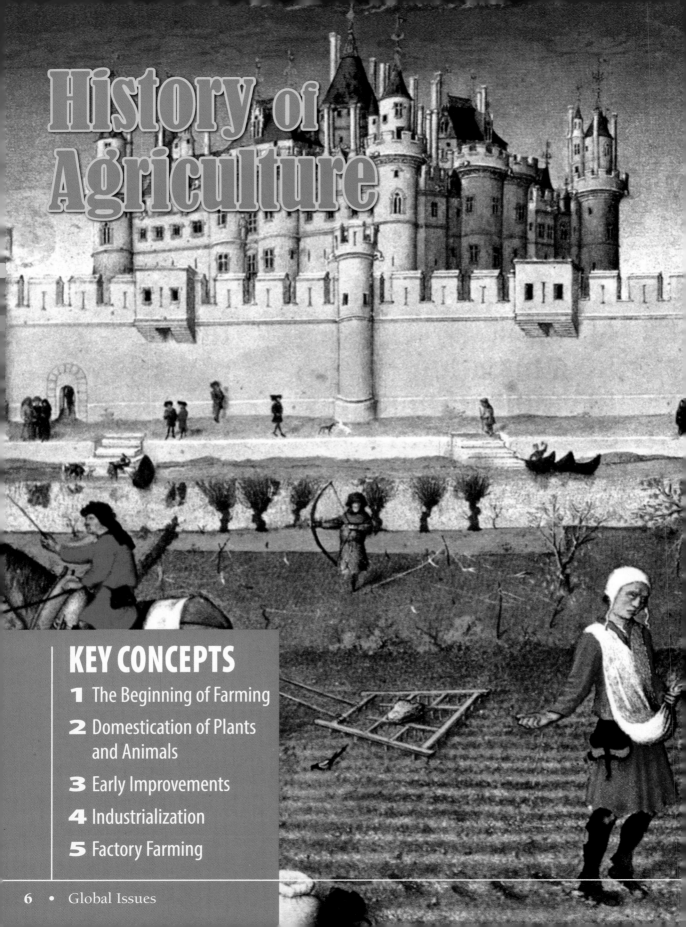

History of Agriculture

KEY CONCEPTS

1 The Beginning of Farming

2 Domestication of Plants and Animals

3 Early Improvements

4 Industrialization

5 Factory Farming

Agriculture has undergone a number of revolutions since it was first developed by humans thousands of years ago. Farming began as simply finding seeds and planting them in the ground. Then, it evolved into **domesticating** both plants and animals. Today, agriculture has become a huge international, industrial business that uses the latest science and technology.

1 The Beginning of Farming

Before the development of farming, humans obtained their food through hunting and gathering. Men hunted animals, while women and children gathered edible nuts and fruits. Finding enough food for everyone was a full-time job. Failure often meant starvation.

Around 12,000 years ago, humans learned that they could have a more secure and reliable food supply if they actually raised plants and animals instead of trying to get them from nature. A number of scholars believe farming first arose in parts of the world at the end of the last **Ice Age**, about 11,000 BC. As the glaciers retreated, the climate in much of the Middle East, South Asia, and China changed from being cool and wet to having long dry periods between rains. This forced many plants to put their energy into seeds rather than woody growth. Areas with an abundance of seeds encouraged permanent human settlement, leading to the planting of seeds and the domestication of animals.

This ensured that people would have a permanent food supply.

Farming laid the groundwork for human civilization. It provided a secure food supply that could be stored for times when harvests were poor. It allowed some peoples to develop other aspects of society such as law, mathematics, writing, and government. The word "civilization" comes from the Latin word *civis*, which means someone who lives in a city. Without farming, it is unlikely that cities, and even civilization, would have developed.

In ancient times as well as today, plows were used to turn over the soil. This loosened the soil and prepared it for the planting of seeds.

Fields were flooded with water to grow rice in ancient China.

2 Domestication of Plants and Animals

An animal becomes domesticated when it is tamed. A plant becomes domesticated when humans use it as part of a crop. When farming began, humans probably selected the wild plants with desirable characteristics, such as the largest fruits or grains. People saved the seeds from these plants and planted them the next year. Eventually, the plants became established crops.

The wild ancestors of wheat, barley, and peas had long existed in the Middle East. There is evidence that farmers in Syria were growing a variety of grains 9,000 years ago. Fig trees may have been planted in the Jordan Valley of the Middle East as early as 11,300 years ago.

In China, people were cultivating rice by 8000 BC. They began raising beans soon after. People in three regions of the Americas independently cultivated corn, squash, potatoes, and sunflowers 10,000 years ago.

Animal domestication happened when humans learned to change the behaviors of animals living in nature. Experts believe that the first animal to be domesticated was the dog, which was bred from wolves. Dogs may have been domesticated in Europe more than 14,000 years ago. By about 6000 BC, cattle, goats, sheep, and pigs were all being raised by farmers along Egypt's Nile Valley and in what is now eastern Turkey, Iraq, and southwestern Iran. Humans domesticated chickens from jungle fowl in parts of Asia 8,000 years ago.

3 Early Improvements

By the beginning of the Bronze Age, about 3000 BC, farming had replaced hunting and gathering in many parts of the world. At the same time, humans made great advances in the science of agriculture. One such advance was intensive farming.

The Sumerians, a people living in what is now Iraq, invented intensive farming around 5000 BC. Intensive farming uses a large amount of labor or other resources on a relatively small area of land. Usually, farmers grow a single crop, such as wheat.

Intensive farming made it possible to support a large population of people who did not farm. This led to the growth of large cities for the first time. Soon, the Egyptians, by using intensive farming in the fertile Nile River Valley, built a large empire.

In ancient China, intensive farming allowed officials to construct a national granary, or warehouse, system. The system allowed them to distribute rice and other grains from places where there were surplus crops to places where there were poor harvests. In what is now Pakistan and India, the Indus Valley Civilization, in the years 5000 to 1500 BC, developed an advanced system of canals and irrigation ditches to supply water to farmlands.

Farming in those ancient times relied entirely on the power of people and animals. People plowed the land using teams of oxen or horses. During the Middle Ages in Europe, from the 5th to the 15th century, farm equipment improved. Farmers use more efficient **scythes** and plows. They also bred powerful draft horses as working animals.

Oxen were used for many agricultural purposes, such as plowing, pulling carts, and powering machines to grind grain.

4 Industrialization

Farming underwent its most rapid change during the Industrial Revolution. The Industrial Revolution, which began in Great Britain in the late 1700s, was characterized by the use of steam power to run machines, the growth of factories, and the mass production of manufactured goods. In 1701, an Englishman, Jethro Tull, invented the seed drill, the first farm machine.

Factory work lured people off the land into cities. This trend continued for hundreds of years. Despite the decline in the rural population, U.S. farm output today is many times higher than it was when most people lived on farms. The primary reason is mechanization, or the invention of machines to do the work of people and animals.

The gasoline engine brought major changes to agriculture in the United States and most of the world. In many regions, it soon became the chief power source for the farm. John Froelich, an Iowa farmer, invented the first successful gasoline tractor in 1892. In 1907, some 600 tractors were in use in the United States, but the number jumped to almost 3.4 million by 1950 and to more than 4.2 million by 2010.

Using the tractor, and later self-propelled machines such as the combine harvester, farmers could do farm tasks much faster and on a greater scale. These advances, plus other innovations, have enabled modern farms in **developed countries** to produce huge amounts of high-quality agricultural products to feed a growing population.

Farm Jobs as a Percent of Total U.S. Jobs, 1790 to 2010

In 1790, 90 percent of Americans lived on farms, but over the past 220 years, the number of Americans employed in farm jobs has steadily declined.

Percent

100 90 80 70 60 50 40 30 20 10 0

1790 1800 1825 1850 1875 1900 1925 1950 1975 2000 2010

Has the Rural-Population Decline Been Harmful to the United States?

The rapid decline of the rural and farm population in the United States has changed the character of the nation. The majority of the U.S. population belonged to farm families from colonial times until the late 19th century. However, as farms mechanized and new opportunities arose elsewhere, more and more people moved from farms to towns and cities. This movement has been called "rural flight."

Farm Families
The smaller rural population has caused problems. There are fewer services in rural areas. Stores and businesses have closed, and we have to drive many miles to shop or visit a doctor.

Government Agriculture Officials
America's farmers are important since they raise so much of our food. However, since there are fewer rural Americans, they have little political power, so their interests are not being addressed.

Economists
People should not complain about the successful growth of mechanized agriculture, even though it results in rural flight. A smaller rural population has not hurt the United States economically.

Agricultural Business Owners
In past times, farming was a difficult, demanding job that often ended in failure. Mechanized agriculture changed that, even if it also led to a decline in the rural population. The trends that led to rural flight have produced larger amounts of food for the entire country.

 For   Supportive   Undecided   Unsupportive   Against

5 Factory Farming

Since the middle of the 20th century, the world demand for meat and animal products has skyrocketed. Between 1967 and 2007, the world's consumption of pork jumped from 33.9 billion tons (30.7 billion tonnes) to almost 100 billion tons (90.7 billion tonnes). In the same time period, consumption of beef increased by 180 percent, eggs by 353 percent, and milk by 711 percent.

The worldwide popularity of fast-food chains has played a leading role in this increased demand for meat and animal products. The only way to meet such demand, while still maintaining standards of quality and taste, is through industrialized agriculture. Most large fast-food companies do not purchase beef from small farmers, which would be very expensive. Instead, big food retailers buy from big producers.

As a result, many farms have become what are called "factory farms." These are huge operations where chickens, cattle, and pigs are kept confined in close quarters. They are raised and processed as if they were on an assembly line.

Feedlots are a typical form of factory farm. Young cattle are brought in and given special feed with easily digestible **nutrients** and **hormones** to make them grow more quickly. In the past, cattle used to be placed in pastures until they reached a certain weight. As they grazed in the fields, they built up muscles. Today, feedlot farmers make sure the cattle do not exercise. This keeps their flesh soft. As for pigs, on factory farms they are fed various chemicals to keep them fat.

Egg production on modern factory farms involves keeping thousands of chickens in small cages under artificial lighting. Each chicken lays about 300 eggs in one year, which is five to ten times as many as an average uncaged chicken. After about a year, when their egg-laying rate slows, the chickens are slaughtered. They are used for soup, pies, or animal feed.

Large pork producers say that pigs that are allowed to roam outdoors, rather than being kept inside on factory farms, may have a greater risk of being contaminated by rodents and diseases they carry.

Do Factory Farms Violate Animal Rights?

O n many large livestock farms, animals are kept in close confinement. Until they are slaughtered, pigs and chickens, in particular, are kept in very tight spaces. Some people feel that such farming is intolerable and should be banned, because they believe animals have a right to live a "natural" life. Other people say that the main concern of livestock farmers should be to keep the animals healthy and to slaughter them humanely. In the United States, laws require that animals be humanely slaughtered.

Animal Rights Activists
Each minute, hundreds of millions of farm animals around the world are murdered for their meat. Billions of others are confined in such tight places that they cannot even turn around. These animals are being denied their basic rights as living things.

Concerned Consumers
Animals have some rights but not necessarily the same rights as people. It is possible that large farms do violate their rights to some extent. Farmers should treat animals in a more humane way.

Restaurant Owners
Animals have the right to not be tortured, but not all livestock farmers torture animals. Animals are raised so that people can eat them. Factory farms also help to keep down the cost of food, which is important to people.

Livestock Farmers
Animal rights critics want everyone to be vegetarians. In general, though, livestock today have a better, healthier, and longer life than they have ever had in nature. Humans have been raising and eating animals for thousands of years, and that is not going to change.

| For | Supportive | Undecided | Unsupportive | Against |

Modern Farm Technology

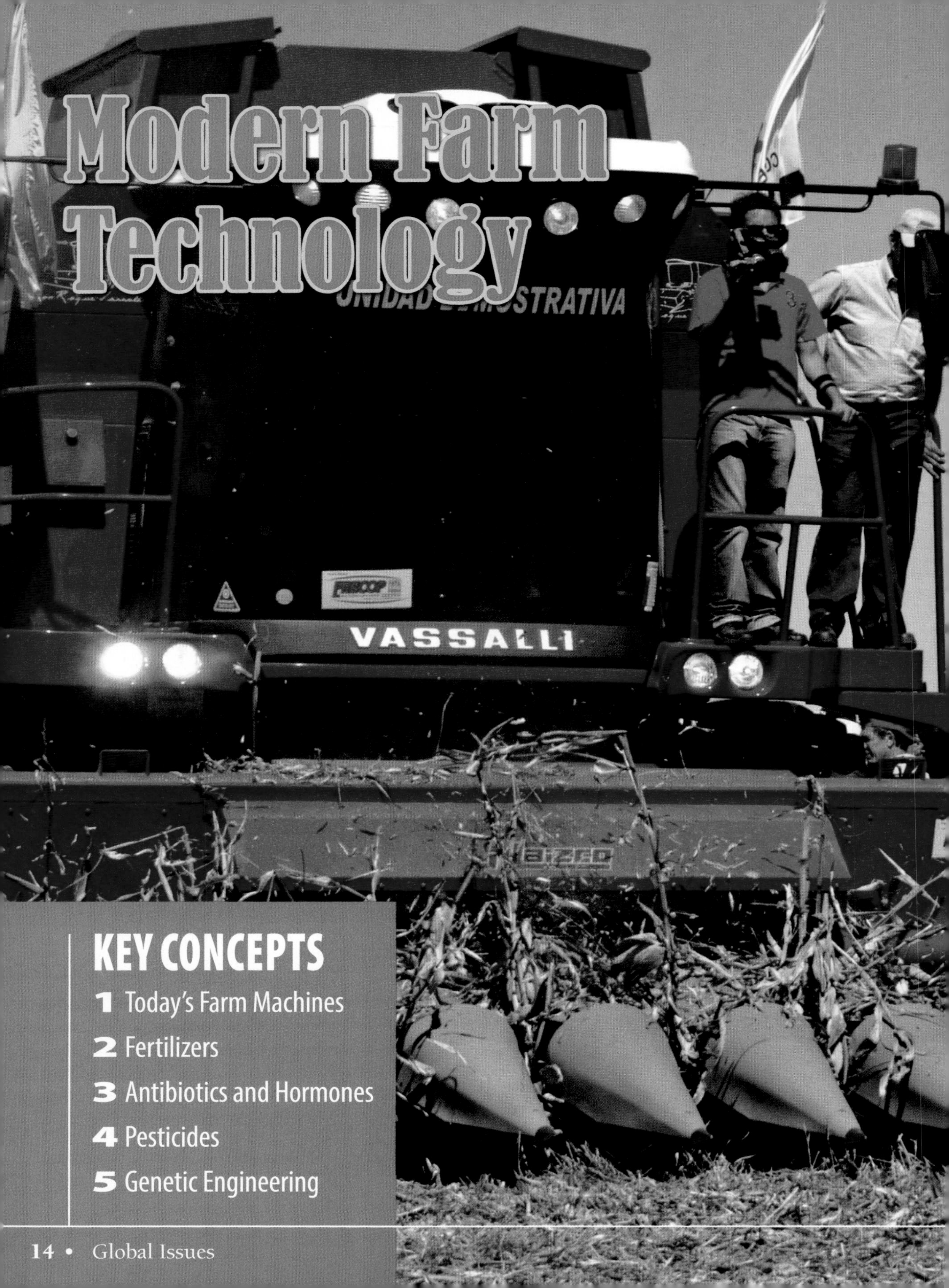

KEY CONCEPTS

1 Today's Farm Machines

2 Fertilizers

3 Antibiotics and Hormones

4 Pesticides

5 Genetic Engineering

Today's big farms use the tools of modern science and technology to raise, harvest, and market plants and animals. Many farmers are more like engineers and technicians in high-tech professions than traditional farmers. Computers and other machines today often allow a single farmer to do what teams of farmers did less than 100 years ago.

1 Today's Farm Machines

As agriculture advanced, the farm industry developed machines to do many types of work, starting with the tractor. Modern tractors run on gasoline, diesel fuel, or liquid propane gas. Tractors come with features such as four-wheel drive, computer-based controls, seat belts, air-conditioned cabs, and **global positioning systems** (GPS). With GPS, farmers can create accurate field maps, keep track of land features, and work when it is raining or dark.

Tractors provide power for a wide range of **tillage** machines. Rotary tillers, which are attached to tractors, loosen soil for planting. Once the soil is loosened, farmers use spreader machines to distribute manure and other fertilizers across plowed fields. After the field has been tilled, farmers use mechanical planters that put the seeds at the precise depth needed. Planters also apply fertilizers, weed killers, and **insecticides**.

Farmers have many machines to help gather crops after they have grown. The most important machine is the combine, or combine harvester, which performs a number of harvesting tasks. It can cut the crop, separate the seed from the plant, and bundle the crop into manageable units. Modern combines have a number of electronic devices, such as a data collector that records every second of operation.

Combines and other farm machines prepare feed for livestock. They also prepare crops for transport, storage, and marketing. Crop dryers, for instance, force dry air through moist grain crops. This allows farmers to harvest wet or moist grain without fear that the grain will spoil while it is in storage.

Combines and other modern farm machines can cost thousands of dollars.

2 Fertilizers

In the past 60 years, world food production has doubled. Much of this increase is due to intensive industrialized farming and modern farm machines. It is also due in part to modern chemical fertilizers that add nutrients to the soil.

Before the Industrial Revolution, all farming was **organic** and depended on the recycling principle of using things over again. Farmers plowed animal manure and dead plants back into the soil. This added nutrients while at the same time getting rid of unwanted waste. Sometimes, farmers also used artificial fertilizers. Some were made from potash, produced by burning vegetable waste, or guano, which is bird droppings.

Today's chemical fertilizers are usually composed of three elements. They are phosphorus, potassium, and **nitrogen**. Nitrogen is most important. Though nitrogen occurs naturally, artificially produced nitrogen compounds, such as nitrates and urea, have proved to be very effective fertilizers. Their discovery during the 1940s transformed agriculture, and crop production increased significantly.

While nitrogen has been a boon to crop production, it has had a harmful effect on the environment. When nitrogen is washed off farmlands by rain and enters rivers, lakes, and eventually the oceans, it stimulates the growth of algae and other plants that live in water. As a result, these plants can grow out of control, taking the oxygen from the water. This creates "dead zones" where fish cannot live because they do not get any oxygen.

Agricultural scientists estimate that the use of fertilizers is responsible for 40 to 60 percent of the increases in crop production seen in recent years.

Should Limits Be Placed on the Use of Chemical Fertilizers?

Farmers now use nine times as much chemical fertilizer as in the 1960s. A further increase of 50 percent is expected over the next 40 years to feed a growing world population. While these fertilizers have made it possible to produce more food, they also have harmful effects. These include contamination of water and an increased risk of some diseases in humans. A 2013 United Nations (UN) report called for a worldwide reassessment of the environmental damage caused by the use of such fertilizers.

Environmentalists
The use of chemical fertilizers should be cut back drastically. Massive use has damaged human health, killed fish, and even contributed to **climate change**.

UN Scientists
The world is facing a fertilizer crisis. Far too much is used in some places, causing environmental damage. Fertilizer use needs to be managed globally.

Farmers
Chemical fertilizer use is already limited somewhat. It is unfortunate that fertilizers result in some environmental damage, but cutting back on their use would badly hurt crop production.

World Agriculture Specialists
Chemical fertilizers are absolutely essential to world food production. Farmers must continue to use them. Even a slight cutback would lead to a sharp increase in world hunger.

For   Supportive   Undecided   Unsupportive   Against

3 Antibiotics and Hormones

Since the 1950s, livestock producers have added low levels of **antibiotics** to the feed and water of healthy cattle, pigs, and chickens. The antibiotics speed the animals' growth. They also prevent infections that tend to occur when animals are housed in crowded and unsanitary conditions. In 2011, drug makers sold nearly 30 million pounds (13.6 million kilograms) of antibiotics for livestock in the United States.

Supporters of antibiotic use say the antibiotics are harmless, improve the health of the animals, and increase food production. Critics, however, say that widespread use of antibiotics poses a danger to humans. They believe that such use could spread "superbugs," or dangerous germs that are resistant to treatment with antibiotics used as medicines.

Groups such as the American Medical Association and the American Public Health Association have called for stopping the use of antibiotics in animals, in order to protect people's health. In December 2013, the U.S. Food and Drug Administration (FDA) took its first steps toward banning the use of certain antibiotics in livestock farming. Farmers and ranchers would not be allowed to use antibiotics to make animals grow bigger. They would also need to get a prescription from a veterinarian for antibiotics to prevent animals from getting sick.

Hormones can make certain cells in the body grow faster. Farmers use specific hormones to make dairy cows produce more milk. They use other hormones to stimulate the growth of cattle that will be slaughtered for meat. The FDA has ruled that the amount of hormones generally given to cattle and dairy cows does not harm the safety of milk or meat that is for human consumption. Some countries have banned hormone use because of suspected harm the hormones may do to cattle, not humans.

Less feed is needed if beef and dairy cattle are given hormones.

4 Pesticides

Farmers use substances called pesticides to prevent, destroy, or control pests such as mice, insects, fungi, weeds, and bacteria that damage crops. Pesticides can be natural substances, such as bacteria that prevent other types of harmful bacteria from attacking crops. They can also be human-made chemicals that kill pests but do not harm plants.

In the past, farmers ground up certain plants, such as tobacco, that they knew kept away insects and sprayed this material on crops. During the 1940s, however, a dramatic change took place in pest control when scientists discovered that they could create pesticides that killed insects and weeds. Since 1945, the use of chemical pesticides has saved much labor and led to huge crop increases around the world.

However, certain pesticides may harm the environment. The widespread use of the pesticide DDT, for example, raised particular concerns. In the 1960s, DDT was found to harm birds, fish, and other types of wildlife. It was also thought to harm people.

Officials banned DDT in the United States in 1972. Later, it was banned throughout much of the world. This has been controversial, since DDT was very effective in killing mosquitoes in **developing countries**. Since the ban, there has been an increase in cases of malaria. This mosquito-borne disease is a serious health issue in some developing countries. The U.S. Environmental Protection Agency (EPA) requires today's pesticides to be **biodegradable** and harmless to humans.

Worldwide Sales of Pesticides

Sales of pesticides have remained fairly stable in North America.
Sales have grown steadily in many other parts of the world.

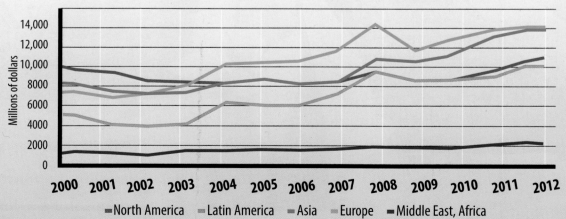

Legend: North America, Latin America, Asia, Europe, Middle East, Africa

5 Genetic Engineering

Genes are structures contained in each cell of every living thing. They carry information that determines how an organism will grow and what characteristics it will have. Scientists have learned how to change the genes of plants to produce desirable traits or eliminate undesirable ones. This is called genetic engineering. Through genetic engineering, scientists have been able to make wheat, corn, and other crops more resistant to drought and pests. This results in larger harvests.

Researchers have also learned to genetically engineer food to improve its nutritional value. An example is golden rice. This is a variety of white rice in which scientists have inserted genes from other plants that produce beta-carotene, a substance found in vegetables. The result is rice that contains vitamin A. Golden rice has proved a health benefit for groups of people who eat a great deal of rice and for whom vitamin A deficiency has been a health problem.

Other types of genetic engineering are taking place in agriculture as well. In 2012, Chinese scientists created a sheep that contained a beneficial type of dietary fat. They combined the sheep's genes with genes taken from a type of roundworm. The result was a sheep with more healthful meat for human consumption.

Foods that have been genetically engineered are called genetically modified, or GM, foods. Genetically modified food is now very common in the United States. About 60 to 70 percent of processed foods on U.S. grocery shelves today have genetically modified ingredients.

More than 90 percent of corn and soybeans in the United States are grown from genetically engineered seeds.

Are GM Foods an Environmental and Health Danger?

O ne of the most controversial issues facing the agriculture industry in the 21st century is the debate over the benefits and dangers of genetically modified food. Many scientists and large **biotechnology** companies claim that increasing the use of GM foods will greatly reduce world hunger. The U.S. government has concluded that GM foods are safe. However, some concerned citizens, scientists, and environmentalists warn that not enough is known yet about the long-term effects of GM foods. They fear that these foods may present risks to health and the environment that will become apparent only in the future.

Environmentalists
We simply do not know enough about GM crops. They could be extremely dangerous. They could interact and breed with weeds to create "superweeds" that would change the entire ecological system that supports all life.

Concerned Consumers
There is reason to be concerned any time scientists experiment with the foods we eat. The companies that sell these foods say that they are safe, but it may be too early to know for sure.

U.S. Government Officials
GM research and GM foods are highly regulated by the government. They have not caused any environmental or health problems. If we were not sure of their safety, we would not allow them to be sold to the public.

GM Scientists
GM crops are completely safe and are already helping hungry people around the world by increasing **crop yields**. GM crops are also being designed to be naturally resistant to a variety of pests. This means that they help the environment by decreasing the use of chemical pesticides.

For   Supportive   Undecided   Unsupportive   Against

The Global Market

KEY CONCEPTS

1 Feeding the World

2 Multinationals

3 Monocropping

4 Farm Trade and Subsidies

5 Sustainable Agriculture

A griculture today is very different from the way it was in the past. In many ways, it is a global enterprise in which large multinational companies have a great deal of influence. These companies, which have operations in more than one country, are involved in many aspects of raising food, from seed production to harvesting to selling in international markets. Not everyone, however, thinks that modern agricultural practices are the best way to produce the world's food supply. As a result of such opinions, **sustainable agriculture** and organic farming are becoming more popular.

1 Feeding the World

Satellite images taken in 2005 show that 40 percent of Earth's land is now used for raising crops and livestock. The images, compiled into a map by scientists at the University of Wisconsin-Madison, show that crop production takes up an area roughly the size of South America. Even more land is used to raise livestock.

Farmland around the world has been increasing for two reasons. They are population growth and the changed nature of world agriculture. In 1700, just 7 percent of land was farmland, and the world's population was about 600 million. Today, the population is above 7 billion. This means that more and more land is needed today to raise more food to feed many more people.

The second reason for the growth in farmland is the position of agriculture in the world today. With the widespread use of pesticides, new fertilizers, and genetically modified seeds, farmers are more efficient in growing crops. They are no longer self-sufficient, however. They are now part of a system that places an emphasis on growing large quantities of crops. They also often depend on large companies for the seeds and other items they need.

"More and more land is needed to raise more food to feed more people."

Today, agriculture is part of a global market. A trip to the supermarket in the United States shows fruits and vegetables from all over the world. One of the biggest farmland expansions in recent years has occurred in Brazil, where huge areas that were once rainforest have been replaced by soybean fields. The soybeans are mainly shipped to China. Farming was once a local industry, but throughout the world today, it has become an international enterprise.

Mapping World Agriculture

North America

Pacific Ocean

Atlantic Ocean

South America

The World's Arable Land

Arable land can be defined as the land area used for crops such as wheat and rice that are replanted year after year. The percentage of land that is arable varies a great deal in different countries. For example, much of the land in some parts of Asia and Africa is not considered arable.

Legend

- 40% or more
- 35–39%
- 30–34%
- 25–29%
- 20–24%
- 15–19%
- 10–14%
- 5–9%
- 0–4%

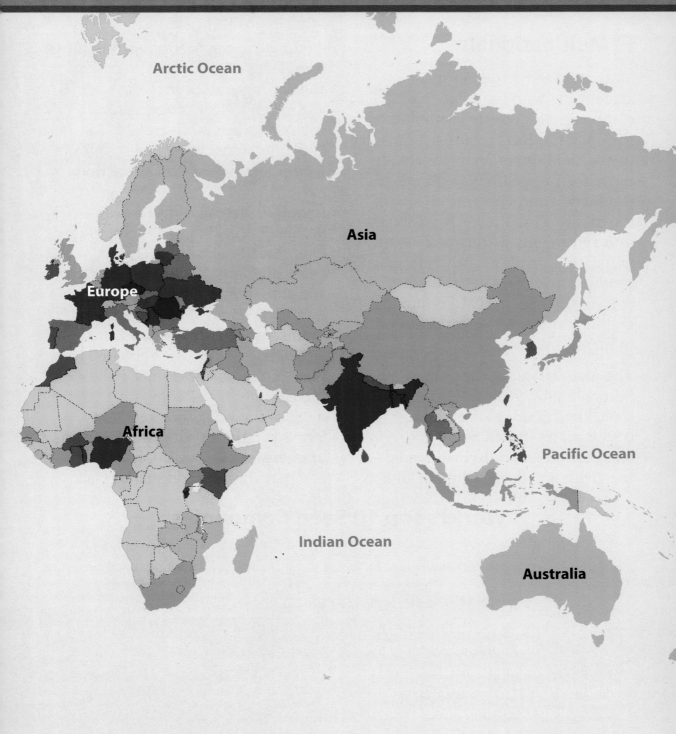

Arctic Ocean

Asia

Europe

Africa

Pacific Ocean

Indian Ocean

Australia

Southern Ocean

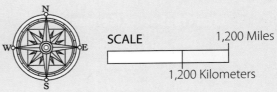

SCALE

1,200 Miles

1,200 Kilometers

2 Multinationals

Many large farmers enter into agreements with multinational companies to produce crops and livestock products that the companies then sell. Multinationals are able to move their operations to places where production and labor are cheapest. In the case of agriculture, they can enter into agreements with farmers in areas with better conditions and cheaper production costs. Multinational corporations such as Monsanto and DuPont now have a great deal of influence over intensive farming.

The grain business, for example, has become highly concentrated, with the United States as the leading country. The United States is the largest producer of **hybrid** seeds, the greatest exporter of grain, and the home to the biggest **agribusiness** companies. U.S. farmers, ranchers, and agribusinesses were the world's leading exporters of agricultural goods between 2000 and 2012. Foreign markets took in a significant part of total U.S. farm production.

About 20 large agribusinesses dominate world agriculture and the food trade today. These large companies are able to grow, process, and ship food more cheaply than traditional family farms. As a result of this, more than 4 million small farms in the United States alone have gone out of business since the 1930s. Increasingly, fewer companies control more of the world market. Many farmers in the developed world turn to intensive farming in order to compete in the world marketplace.

World's Top 10 Seed Companies

A small number of companies sell most of the seeds used by farmers worldwide. The top 10 companies account for about three-quarters of the world market.

Company (headquarters)	Market Share in 2013
Monsanto (USA)	26.0%
DuPont/Pioneer (USA)	18.2%
Syngenta (Switzerland)	9.2%
Vilmorin/Groupe Limagrain (France)	4.8%
Land O' Lakes/WinField (USA)	3.9%
KWS AG (Germany)	3.6%
Bayer CropScience (Germany)	3.3%
Dow AgroSciences (USA)	3.1%
Sakata (Japan)	1.6%
Takii & Company (Japan)	1.6%

Is Farming Unfairly Controlled by a Few Agribusiness Companies?

To a large extent, a few agribusiness companies, led by Monsanto, Archer Daniels Midland, and DuPont, now play a major role in world agriculture. In effect, they control the market for seeds, fertilizers, pesticides, and the distribution of harvests. They are also major **lobbyists** for **farm subsidies** in the United States, Europe, and Japan. Farmers in both developed countries and developing countries often rely on these companies for growing and marketing crops.

Organic Farmers
The big agribusinesses control everything in farming. They are concerned only about the big farm operations and making a profit. They influence government policies, which often do not help organic farmers. It is hard for us to compete with them since they can sell products at lower prices.

Small Family Farmers
All farmers, big and small, benefit from the work of the big agribusinesses, which help in improving seeds, making better fertilizers, and getting us government subsidies. The downside is that they make many decisions that small farmers used to make for themselves.

Owners of Large Farms
Agribusinesses have been a tremendous help to big farmers. They have increased the effectiveness of large operations and lowered the costs of raising crops and livestock.

Large Feedlot Owners
The large agribusinesses produce nutritious and affordable feed used in feedlot operations. Without this feed, we could not raise the amount of meat we produce, which is needed to feed a growing world population.

| For | Supportive | Undecided | Unsupportive | Against |

3 Monocropping

When European countries established **colonies** in Latin America, Africa, and Asia, beginning in the late 1400s, they developed plantation economies. A plantation is a large area of land that employs local workers to cultivate a single **commercial crop**. The practice is called monocropping. Today, most colonies are independent countries. However, many areas of the world are still heavily dependent on monocropping. The same crop is grown year after year, without resting the soil or practicing **crop rotation**. Monocrops today include sugarcane, tea, coffee, cocoa, and cotton.

The benefit of monocropping is that it allows farmers to concentrate on one particular crop. That means that they can invest in machinery, pesticides, and fertilizers designed specifically for that crop. However, monocropping has its problems. A fall in the price of a monocrop or a crop disease that wipes out the harvest can cause great hardship for farmers. In a country dependent on one crop, thousands of people can be thrown into poverty. Monocropping can also remove nutrients from the soil and make plants more vulnerable to disease.

Critics of monocropping advocate greater use of mixed farming, where the farmer grows a number of different crops. This type of farming was once common around the world. Mixed farming was a safeguard against financial ruin if a single crop failed.

The largest corn harvest in U.S. history was predicted in 2012, but excessive heat and drought resulted in a harvest that was 27 percent below the forecast.

4 Farm Trade and Subsidies

Before the Industrial Revolution, most trade in food products was local. People ate food that they grew themselves or that was grown nearby and transported only short distances, to be sold in the marketplaces of nearby towns and villages. Trade over longer distances was often limited to wine and dried products such as grains and spices. Trade in salt, sugar, coffee, and cocoa helped to build the wealth of Western Europe.

When canning and refrigerated ships, railroad cars, and trucks became available, the trade in food rapidly expanded. Today, even fresh fruits and vegetables are routinely shipped around the globe. In the United States, food now travels an average of 1,240 miles (2,000 kilometers) from farm to plate.

The world trade in farm products today is so huge and so important that governments have acted to protect farmers. Governments want to make sure that farmers are not ruined financially if crop prices or yields fall because of oversupply, drought, or other reasons. Both the United States and the **European Union** spend billions of dollars each year on farm subsidies. Such subsidies are usually in the form of government payments to farmers, low-cost loans, lower taxes, or other monetary aid.

U.S. Agricultural Exports, 2012

(in billions of dollars)

The United States sells food to many countries. More than 50 percent of U.S. agricultural exports are shipped to China, Canada, Mexico, and Japan.

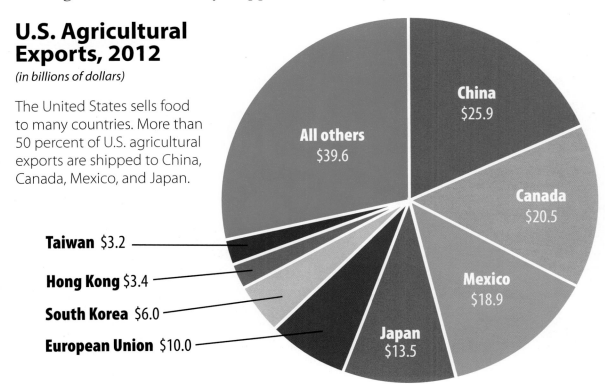

Taiwan $3.2
Hong Kong $3.4
South Korea $6.0
European Union $10.0

All others $39.6
China $25.9
Canada $20.5
Mexico $18.9
Japan $13.5

5 Sustainable Agriculture

Some people are concerned that factory farms and industrial agriculture are depleting the soil and harming the environment. In response, since the 1990s, the sustainable agriculture movement has grown around the world. Organic farms are at the center of sustainable agriculture. Crops and livestock grown or raised on organic farms are produced naturally and with minimal impact on the environment.

These farms avoid using chemical pesticides and fertilizers. Instead, they use natural substances, such as **compost** and manure, as fertilizers. The number of organic farms in the United States increased from about 6,600 in 2000 to nearly 13,000 in 2011. Foods grown on organic farms, which can be bought in most U.S. supermarkets, are becoming more popular, even though they are generally more expensive than non-organic foods.

Another development in the sustainable agriculture movement is community-supported agriculture, or CSA. CSA connects local farmers with local consumers. Consumers cover a farm's yearly operating expenses by purchasing a share of the season's harvest. Members help pay for seeds, fertilizer, water, labor, and equipment repair. In return, the farm provides them with fresh, high-quality produce. There are now thousands of CSA farms in the United States and Canada.

More than $30 billion in organic food was sold in the United States in 2012.

Does the U.S. Government Unfairly Promote Agribusiness over Sustainable and Organic Farming?

Large agribusinesses have a great deal of influence on the U.S. government. They try to persuade lawmakers to pass policies that favor them. The government gives these businesses subsidies and other types of financial help. Some people think the government unfairly supports agribusinesses over small family farms, sustainable farms, and organic farms.

Owners of Small Farms

The federal government pays more attention to the needs of the big agribusinesses than to small farms. It is difficult for small farms to compete against these businesses, especially when the U.S. government favors them.

Supermarket Shoppers

Most people buy food that mainly comes from the efforts of agribusinesses that keep food costs down by mass production. People care about costs. However, if the government provided more help for organic farmers, organic foods might be less expensive.

Politicians from Farming States

It is not a question of fairness. It is a question of efficient food production. The big farms and big businesses receive the support they do because they do a better job of feeding the world.

Agribusiness Executives

People criticize the agribusinesses because they are so large. They do not realize that agriculture has changed. Small family farms and organic farms cannot feed the world any more. Government helps agribusinesses because these businesses succeed.

  For Supportive Undecided Unsupportive Against

Future of Agriculture

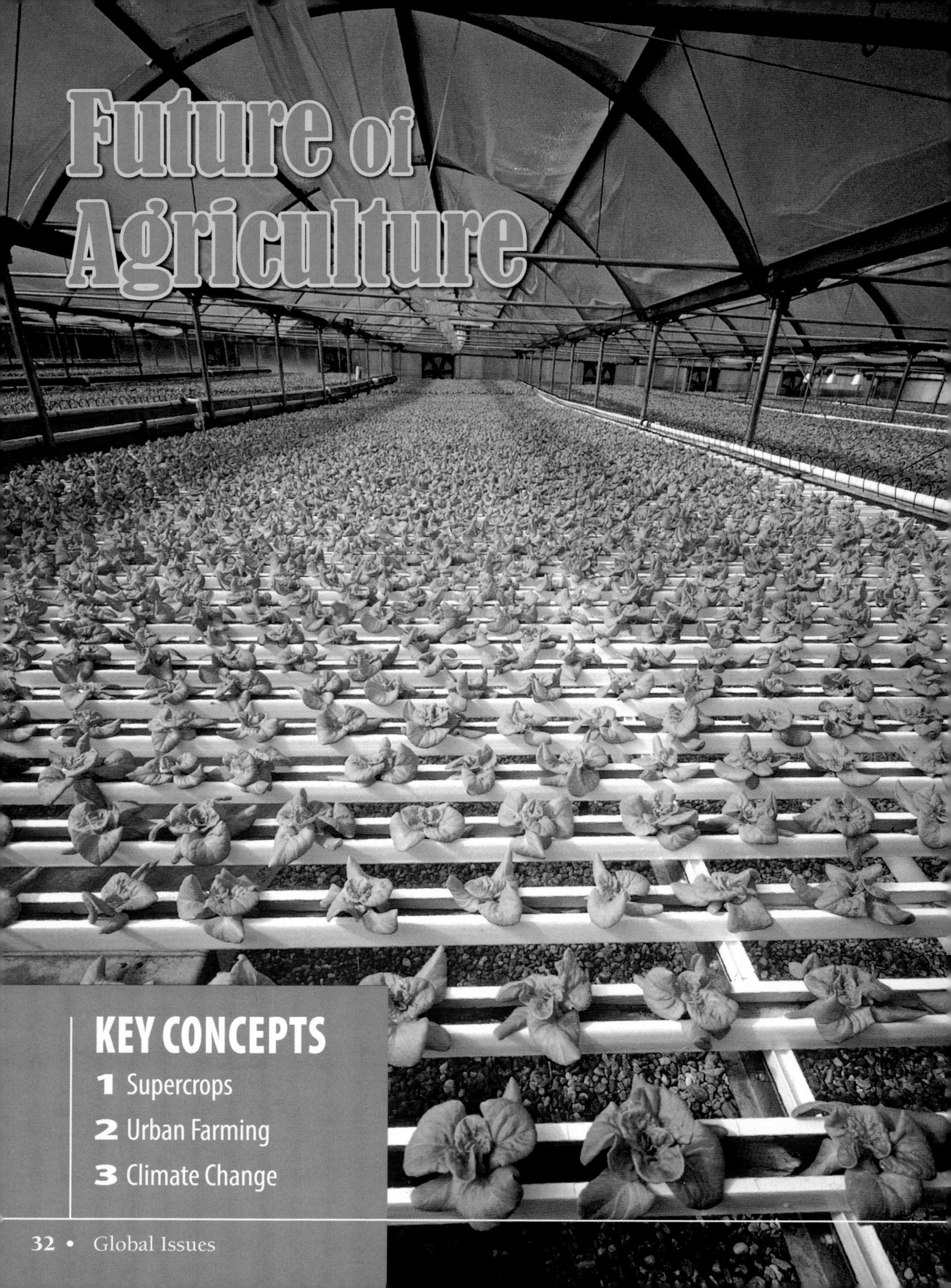

KEY CONCEPTS

1 Supercrops

2 Urban Farming

3 Climate Change

What will happen to agriculture in the future? At present, farmers are able to grow enough food to feed the world. Concerns have been raised, however, regarding whether farmers will continue to be able to feed an expanding world population, which is expected to reach 9.6 billion by 2050. Science holds out promise that the answer is yes, but climate change may pose significant problems.

1 Supercrops

Scientists are working on new genetically modified "supercrops." They are adding genes to crops such as wheat or corn that cause the plants to make their own pesticides. These substances within a plant would kill or drive away common insect pests that tried to eat it. Scientists have also developed genetically engineered plants that make their own nitrogen fertilizer by taking nitrogen out of the air and depositing it in the soil. This would eliminate the need for some chemical fertilizers.

Agricultural scientists are working on genetically modifying plants so that they can take in more energy from the Sun for **photosynthesis**. This would allow the plants to grow bigger and faster. Crops may also be developed that can grow more than once. This would take away the need for farmers to plow the soil and plant new seeds. Farmland that is not very productive could benefit if scientists succeed in developing plants that can survive drought. Scientists are also working on flood-resistant plants.

2 Urban Farming

A number of agricultural experts say that one way to increase the world food supply might be urban agriculture. Urban agriculture involves growing plants and raising animals in and around cities. It features many types of production systems, including traditional open gardens, protected environments, and **hydroponic** greenhouses. Instead of transporting food from farms into cities by truck, food could be grown in tall urban greenhouses.

Indoor farming goes by many names, such as all-season farming, undercover agronomy, and controlled environment agriculture, or CEA. People are already converting unused factories, warehouses, office buildings, and other facilities into urban farms. Many are building new glass greenhouses that use a combination of natural sunlight and powerful artificial lights. World vegetable production in greenhouses reached a major milestone in 2012, when the total area used was more than 1 million acres (404,600 hectares) for the first time.

3 Climate Change

The word "climate" describes the typical weather conditions for a large area over a long period of time. Many scientists believe Earth's climate is currently changing. Average temperatures are becoming warmer, leading to such developments as melting polar ice caps, rising sea levels, more powerful hurricanes, and more destructive tornadoes. According to some scientists, climate change will have a major impact on farming and Earth's food supply.

Despite scientific and technological advances, agriculture today still remains dependent on climate. In many areas, growing crops successfully depends on patterns of rainfall. In the past, rainfall has generally been neither too little nor too much, on average, over long periods. This has enabled the world's major farming regions to provide the planet with a regular food supply. Some scientists say that climate change could end that reliability. Areas that are now farmland could turn into deserts, and deserts could turn into wetlands. Seacoasts could be flooded. Such changes have happened in the past. For example, Africa's vast Sahara Desert, one of the driest places on Earth, was a lush wetland around 12,000 years ago.

Many scientists believe that a major challenge for farmers and world governments in the coming years will be how to deal with climate change. It may be possible to deal with some of the effects by expanding farm irrigation systems. Scientists may be able to develop crops that can better withstand long dry or wet periods. It might also be necessary to plant crops on land that is not currently being used as farmland, such as forestland. However, there is no one answer to solving the problems caused by climate change.

Rising sea levels and flooding from climate change could reduce the amount of farmland in coastal areas of the world.

Is Climate Change a Serious Threat to Agriculture?

According to some scientists, climate change in the coming years could pose a serious risk to world agriculture. They point out that rising temperatures could reduce agricultural production by about 2 percent each decade during the 21st century. Other scientists believe that, in some parts of the world, certain aspects of climate change could be beneficial. They think that higher levels of carbon dioxide in the air, which makes temperatures rise, could help plants grow, since plants use carbon dioxide to make their own food.

Some Climate Scientists
Climate change poses a serious risk to food supplies. It will cause crop production to drop and prices to rise, while the demand for food will increase because of population growth.

Agricultural Experts
Climate change seems to be already having an impact on agriculture. In some parts of the world, crop production has gone down in recent years.

Some Citizens
Climate change is beyond my control. As long as enough food is being produced worldwide, it does not seem that there is anything to be concerned about.

Skeptical Scientists
There is reason to believe that climate change may help agriculture. In some parts of the world, crop production could actually increase. This would offset losses in other areas.

For   Supportive   Undecided   Unsupportive   Against

Agriculture through History

Few human activities have changed as much as farming has over the past 13,000 years. These changes have resulted in an increased supply of food. Without those changes, the human population would be much smaller than it is today.

11,000 BC
Farming begins in several parts of the world.

5000 BC
The Sumerians develop intensive farming.

AD 1701
Jethro Tull invents the seed drill, the first agricultural machine.

1790
About 90 percent of the U.S. population lives on farms.

1892

1793
Eli Whitney patents the cotton gin, which separated cotton fibers from cotton seeds. This device led to a major increase in cotton farming.

1870
Farmers account for less than 50 percent of workers in the United States for the first time in the country's history.

1892
John Froelich invents the gasoline-powered tractor.

1906
Congress passes the Meat Inspection Act to make sure that meat being sold is safe to eat.

1701

1943
The pesticide DDT is introduced in the United States.

1950
Tractors outnumber horses on U.S. farms.

1972
The U.S. government bans the use of DDT. It is later banned in much of the world as well.

1990
Congress passes the Organic Food Production Act, requiring the U.S. Department of Agriculture (USDA) to develop standards for organically produced products.

2011

1990

2011
Drug makers sell nearly 30 million pounds (13.6 million kg) of antibiotics to be used in livestock in the United States.

2012
Chinese scientists create a genetically modified sheep by combining the animal's genes with roundworm genes, to produce meat that is more healthful for people to eat.

2013
The FDA begins to take steps to ban the widespread use of certain antibiotics in cows, chicken, and pigs being raised for meat.

2013

Careers in Agriculture

AGRONOMIST

Duties Responsible for the successful growth of crops by selecting seeds, fertilizers, and harvesting techniques that ensure the highest quality

Education A bachelor's degree in science with agronomy or plant production as a major area of study

Interest Science, working with plants, solving problems, and working outdoors

Agronomists work in a variety of settings, including outdoors on farms collecting soil and plant data, in an office, and in a laboratory analyzing data. These diverse working conditions allow agronomists to effectively study the interaction of plants and soils, as well as find ways to improve the quality and yield of agricultural crops. This field of study, sometimes referred to as crop science, plant science, or soil science, also involves other practices such as irrigating, harvesting, and soil grading. Many agronomists are also farmers. Others work as consultants for large agricultural companies to develop improved farming methods.

ORGANIC FARMER

Duties Produces food without the use of synthetic fertilizers, pesticides, and drugs

Education A graduate degree in organic horticulture or agriculture

Interest Human health, the environment, and food production

Organic farmers must be committed to producing agricultural crops using methods that protect the environment and do not involve chemical fertilizers or pesticides. Organic food growers must meet U.S. government standards in order to market their products as "certified organic." To maintain certification, farmers must practice long-term soil management, prevent pesticide contamination from nearby farms, and keep detailed farm records. They must also meet standards for cleanliness, storage, and pest control as stated in the Organic Food Production Act, which was passed in 1990.

RANCHER

Duties The care and production of livestock

Education Training received on the job, in addition to a bachelor's degree in farm management or applied agricultural technology and entrepreneurship

Interest A passion for raising animals and a willingness to start and run a business

A rancher is a farmer who raises cattle, horses, or other livestock on large areas of grazing land. One of the most important tasks is monitoring the quality of range grasses consumed by livestock. Careful recording of grass quality ensures the well-being of livestock and prevents the **overgrazing** of valuable ranch grasslands. Another important aspect of ranching is caring for the health of livestock herds. Ranchers routinely vaccinate their animals against disease and provide medical attention when they are ill.

PLANT SCIENTIST

Duties Using biotechnology to develop new and improved varieties of plants

Education A master's degree in biological science or botany

Interest A passion for working with plants and biotechnology

Plant scientists work with biotechnology to develop new plant strains by altering a plant's genetic material. This specialized field of genetic engineering involves a complex process of extracting the genetic material from healthy plant cells to create new plants with improved traits. A major goal of plant science is to produce plant strains that grow larger or faster and that have increased resistance to pests and disease. Plant scientists may be self-employed or work as researchers in universities, large biotechnology corporations, or non-profit organizations, such as the UN's Food and Agriculture Organization (FAO).

Key Agricultural Organizations

USDA

Goal Develop and put into effect U.S. government policy concerning agriculture, forestry, and food

Reach United States

Facts Established by President Abraham Lincoln on May 15, 1862

The United States Department of Agriculture (USDA) contains numerous divisions or bureaus, most of which are responsible for assisting farmers in solving farm problems. Several bureaus have programs to help farmers financially. The USDA actively helps state farm bureaus with agricultural policy and regulates both the growing of food and the care of livestock. The USDA is also responsible for the enforcement of agricultural laws that are passed by Congress and signed by the president.

FAO

Goal Lead international efforts to defeat hunger

Reach Worldwide

Facts An agency of the United Nations that was founded in 1945

The Food and Agriculture Organization (FAO) is one of the largest agencies of the United Nations. It has more than 190 member countries and a budget of $1 billion per year. The FAO carries out hundreds of projects all over the world to improve food production. Since the early 1960s, FAO efforts have reduced the proportion of hungry people in developing countries from more than 50 percent to less than 20 percent. The organization also encourages sustainable agriculture and rural development as long-term strategies for increasing food production and food security, while conserving natural resources.

FFA

Goal Provide young people with vocational training in agriculture

Reach United States

Facts More than 7,570 chapters in all 50 states, Puerto Rico, and the Virgin Islands

The National FFA Organization grew out of the Smith-Hughes Act of 1917, which established government-sponsored agricultural courses in public high schools. It became a formal organization in 1928. At the time, it was called the Future Farmers of America. The name was changed to the National FFA Organization in 1988 to reflect the growing diversity of agriculture. Members of the FFA today participate in vocational training programs that include all aspects of farm production and management and all phases of today's agribusiness. These include forestry, soil conservation, computer operation, wildlife management, and livestock farming.

NLPA

Goal Provide a public voice for American livestock farmers

Reach United States and Canada

Facts Represents more than 215,000 farmers and ranchers involved in animal agriculture

The National Livestock Producers Association (NLPA) was founded in 1921 to help ranchers and other livestock farmers expand their markets and to lobby government on behalf of livestock farming. The NLPA both promotes livestock production and helps promote new ideas in livestock farming. It also represents the interests of livestock farmers before federal agencies and Congress. In addition, the NLPA acts like a bank, lending money to livestock producers to expand their operations.

Research an Agricultural Issue

The Issue

Farming today and in the future is a subject of much debate. People disagree about issues such as whether intensive mechanized farming should be expanded or sustainable and organic farming should be supported instead. It is important to enter into a discussion to hear all the points of view before making decisions. Discussing issues will ensure that the actions taken are beneficial for all involved.

Get The Facts

Choose an issue (Political, Cultural, Economic, or Ecological) from this book. Then, pick one of the four groups presented in the issue spectrum. Using the book and research in the library or on the Internet, find out more about its point of view. What is important to members of the group? Why is it backing or opposing the particular issue? What claims or facts can it use to support its point of view? Be sure to write clear and concise supporting arguments for your group. Focus on agriculture and the way the group's needs relate to it. Will this group be affected in a positive or negative way by action taken related to agriculture?

Use the Concept Web

A concept web is a useful research tool. Read the information and review the structure in the concept web on the next page. Use the relationships between concepts to help you understand your group's point of view.

Organize Your Research

Sort your information into organized points. Make sure your research clearly answers what impact the issue will have on your chosen group, how that impact will affect it, and why the group has chosen its specific point of view.

AGRICULTURE CONCEPT WEB

Use this concept web to understand the network of factors involved in agricultural issues.

- Environmentally friendly
- Produces food without the use of chemicals

- Factory farms
- The norm in the developed world
- Increasing in the developing world
- Fewer people can produce more food
- Relies on external inputs, such as seeds, fertilizers, and pesticides

- Self-sufficient
- Produces a variety of crops and raises a range of livestock

Organic Farming

Intensive Farming

Mixed Farming

AGRICULTURE

Chemical Agents

Biotechnology

Hunger

- Herbicides
- Pesticides

- Genetic engineering
- Concerns over long-term effects

- Need for adequate food supply
- Possible impact of climate change

Test Your Knowledge

Answer each of the questions below to test your knowledge about the future of farming.

1 Before farming, how did humans obtain food?

2 What was the first step in the historical development of farming?

3 Who first developed intensive farming?

4 Approximately what percent of the world's land is farmland?

5 What is the term used for large operations where pigs, cattle, and chickens are raised and processed as if they were on an assembly line?

6 What is a large machine that performs several harvesting jobs?

7 What is the average distance that food travels from farm to consumer in the United States?

8 What is the most important element in most fertilizers?

9 What is the most important characteristic of raising crops on a plantation farm?

10 What is the name given to a genetically modified rice that contains a large amount of vitamin A?

Key Words

agribusiness: a company involved in some aspect of agriculture as a large-scale business operation, such as the manufacturing and selling of farm machinery, equipment, and supplies or the processing, storing, and selling of farm products

antibiotics: drugs that are used to kill bacteria

biodegradable: capable of decomposing naturally

biotechnology: the use of living organisms to manufacture products

climate change: a change in average temperatures and other weather conditions over a long period of time, such as the major warming trend that many scientists agree has been taking place over the past century

colonies: territories that are separate from but that are governed by a ruling country

commercial crop: a crop grown to be sold rather than used by the farmer

compost: decaying organic matter used as a fertilizer

crop rotation: the practice of growing different crops in succession on the same land

crop yields: quantities of crops produced in a single growing season

developed countries: countries that have undergone the process of industrialization

developing countries: countries with low average income that until recently had little manufacturing and technology

domesticating: taming an animal or cultivating a plant for human use

European Union: a single market of 28 European nations

farm subsidies: financial aid given by a government to an individual company or farm owner

fertilizers: substances added to soil to help plants grow better

global positioning systems: systems that use signals from satellites to tell locations

hormones: substances produced in a body that control growth and development

hybrid: in agriculture, a plant that is produced from a cross between two different plants in order to produce higher yields

hydroponic: related to the process of growing plants in sand, gravel, or liquid with added nutrients, but without soil

Ice Age: a period during which Earth's climate was cold and much of Earth was covered with ice

insecticides: substances used to destroy insects

lobbyists: people who aim to influence public officials

nitrogen: a gas that makes up the majority of Earth's atmosphere and is important for plant growth

nutrients: substances that living things need to grow and live

organic: coming from living things

overgrazing: allowing animals to graze to the point where the land and vegetation are damaged

photosynthesis: the process used by plants to convert energy from sunlight into food

scythes: tools used for cutting crops such as grass or wheat, with a long curved blade

sustainable agriculture: a method of farming that attempts to minimize damage to the environment

tillage: preparing and cultivating soil, for example by plowing

Index

agribusinesses 26, 27, 31
agronomists 38
animal rights 13
antibiotics 18, 37

biotechnology 20, 21, 39

civilization 7
climate change 17, 33, 34, 35
combines 10, 15
community-supported agriculture 30
consumers and shoppers 21, 30, 31
corn 8, 20, 33
crops 8, 9, 15, 16, 19, 20, 23, 28, 33, 34, 35

DDT 19, 37
domestication of plants and animals 7, 8

environment 16, 17, 19, 21, 30
Europe 8, 9, 10, 29

factory farms 12, 13, 30
fast-food industry 12
feedlots 12, 27
fertilizers 15, 16, 17, 30, 33
Food and Agriculture Organization 39, 40
Food and Drug Administration 18, 37
Froelich, John 10, 36
Future Farmers of America 41

genetic engineering 20, 21, 33, 37, 39
genetically modified foods 20, 21, 33
globalization 23, 29

history of agriculture 7, 8, 9, 10, 16, 36, 37
hormones 12, 18
hunger 21, 34, 35
hybrid seeds 26

Ice Age 7
Industrial Revolution 10, 29

insecticides 15
intensive farming 9, 26

livestock 8, 12, 13, 18, 23, 30, 39, 41

machinery 10, 13, 15 , 16, 36
meat 12, 18, 27
monocropping 28
multinationals 23, 26

National Livestock Producers Association 41
nitrogen 16, 33

organic farming 16, 23, 27, 30, 37, 38
organic foods 30, 37, 38

pesticides 19, 21, 30, 33
plantations 28
plant scientists 39
population growth 23, 33

ranchers 39
rice 8, 9, 20
rural population 10, 11

seeds 7, 8, 15, 23, 36
subsidies 27, 29
sustainable agriculture 23, 30, 31

tractors 10, 15, 36, 37
Tull, Jethro 10, 36

United Nations 17, 39, 40
United States 10, 11, 18, 19, 20, 21, 26, 29, 30, 31, 40
United States Department of Agriculture 37, 40
urban agriculture 33

vegetarians 13

wheat 8, 9, 20, 33

Log on to www.av2books.com

AV[2] by Weigl brings you media enhanced books that support active learning. Go to www.av2books.com, and enter the special code found on page 2 of this book. You will gain access to enriched and enhanced content that supplements and complements this book. Content includes video, audio, weblinks, quizzes, a slide show, and activities.

AV[2] Online Navigation

Audio
Listen to sections of the book read aloud.

Book Pages
AV[2] pages directly correspond to pages in the book.

Key Words
Study vocabulary, and complete a matching word activity.

Quizzes
Test your knowledge.

Slide Show
View images and captions, and prepare a presentation.

Video
Watch informative video clips.

Embedded Weblinks
Gain additional information for research.

Try This!
Complete activities and hands-on experiments.

AV[2] was built to bridge the gap between print and digital. We encourage you to tell us what you like and what you want to see in the future.

Sign up to be an AV[2] Ambassador at www.av2books.com/ambassador.

Due to the dynamic nature of the Internet, some of the URLs and activities provided as part of AV[2] by Weigl may have changed or ceased to exist. AV[2] by Weigl accepts no responsibility for any such changes. All media enhanced books are regularly monitored to update addresses and sites in a timely manner. Contact AV[2] by Weigl at 1-866-649-3445 or av2books@weigl.com with any questions, comments, or feedback.